NO EXIT!
GOD SAID,
RELEASED!

Leandra Soto

No Exit! God Said, Released!

© 2024 by Leandra Soto

This edition has been published by Revive Publishers
New York, United States of America
www.editorialrevive.com

Printed in the United States of America
First Edition: December, 2024

Editorial Revive is a division of Revive Group LLC

DEDICATION

To my Lord and Savior, who delivered me from every painful past memory, wound, rejection, insecurity, and fear.

To every child who has endured any kind of abuse. To any man or woman whose inner child is still screaming from those past traumatic memories as a child.

To my husband, children, family, friends, and church family, whom I love dearly—may they always remember that with the Lord by their side, they have nothing to fear.

To all who have supported this book, may the Lord bless you with a double portion.

Isaiah 41:10

"Fear not, for I am with you; be not dismayed, for I am your God; I will strengthen you, I will help you, I will uphold you with my righteous right hand."

PREFACE

In this book, I share my life experiences as a child, teenager, and young woman, along with the profound impact they had on my life. I reflect on the circumstances I had no control over and the wrong choices I made, as well as the unhealthy memories that flooded my mind, heart, and soul—memories I struggled to let go of.

Through these pages, I invite you to see that you do not have to be trapped by a past that cannot be changed. There is hope in Jesus Christ. He offers a second chance to live as though you had never experienced abuse, unforeseen trauma, heartache, wounds, pain, depression, loneliness, suicidal thoughts, or any other affliction.

My prayer for you, as you read this book, is that you will release all that has afflicted your life and let go of the damage it has caused you mentally, emotionally, and physically. May you find the courage to lay it all to rest, so you can flourish as you were always meant to—since the foundation of the earth.

Know this: your past no longer has the power to cripple your future, because you no longer live there. May this book help you embrace that truth and realize it is time for a fresh start.

Exodus 8:1

"And the Lord spoke to Moses, 'Go to Pharaoh and say to him, "Thus says the Lord: LET MY PEOPLE GO, that they may serve Me."

TABLE OF CONTENT

Chapters

Chapter 1

The Birth

Psalm 139:14

"I will praise You; for I am fearfully and wonderfully made; Marvelous are Your works, And that my soul knows very well."

Birth is so beautiful. The thought of an unborn baby growing inside of a woman is a miracle in itself. The new arrival will bring so much love and joy, it is overwhelming. Parents are filled with so much expectation and so many plans.

Psalm 139:14–16 (NKJV) says:

"I will praise You, for I am fearfully and wonderfully made; Marvelous are Your works, And that my soul knows very well.

My frame was not hidden from You, when I was made in secret, And skillfully wrought in the lowest parts of the earth.

Your eyes saw my substance, being yet unformed. And in Your book they all were written, The days fashioned for me, When as yet there were none of them."

These are very powerful scriptures. They make so much sense to the one being born, with all the anticipation and love awaiting them. How wonderfully blessed are those who experience such a welcoming.

Unfortunately, every birth is not like the one I described above, and not all welcoming experiences are the same.

Today, even as I am writing this book, there are babies being born to parents who will reject them—even from the womb. Parents dealing with addictions, sexual perversions, poverty, or other issues that will have a great negative impact on the baby coming into this new world. This will raise a question mark over their future as they grow.

It happened to me many times—questioning:

Why was I born if I was going to have to endure hardship, abuse, neglect, rejection, or chaos?

Faced with so many unanswered questions, I struggled to understand my purpose.

I want to clarify that my own birth was one of being welcomed into this new world by many. Everyone was filled with excitement, ready to meet this precious baby girl—at least, that is what I was told. How beautiful to know that love was awaiting! My mom was full of joy, along with my biological father.

I also had a grandma who, in time, would come and steal me away from my parents, just to pour her love upon this precious little gift. And that gift was me! I had nothing to worry about, at least in those moments. I was loved, safe, and secure. I just needed to be the cute, adorable infant I was meant to be—like the many, many other precious babies being born today.

It's so important how we receive the one being born. Did you know that the first five years of a child's developmental life are so very important, according to **HHS.GOV**, for their health and well-being? Those are the years in which a child is being "framed."

So, it would seem that I had nothing to worry about in this new world—never realizing that my fate was awaiting in the near future. But not by the hands that received me at birth or by the loving God in heaven, but by an individual who would take advantage of a vulnerable, innocent life. All because he accepted the welcoming invitation of someone looking for love after a hurtful breakup—my mom.

As an infant, I simply needed to take in and enjoy the pleasant moments of the *now*.

Every child's environment will have a lasting impact. So, how will this newborn remember those beautiful early moments—of being an infant, a toddler, or during early childhood—if one day they will be overshadowed by so many haunting memories?

I once read how important the environment is for a child. For example:

- If a child is born into an environment where all kinds of dysfunction are happening, they will likely begin to believe that dysfunction is normal until shown otherwise.
- If a child lives with hostility, they learn to fight.
- If a child lives with ridicule, they learn to be shy.
- If a child lives with shame, they learn to feel guilty.

But:

- If a child lives with encouragement, they learn confidence.

- If a child lives with security, they learn to have faith.
- If a child lives with tolerance, they learn to be patient. (*Dorothy Law Nolte*)

My birth started off with so much enthusiasm, with love and nurturing that was filled with security. There were so many possibilities of a mighty, purposeful future. Why wouldn't there be?

But all the stories to come will validate the joy that awaited this baby girl.

Every story is different. Some individuals are tremendously blessed by the amazing memories of their upbringing, and my heart rejoices for them. Any human being born into this world should have the absolute best in every aspect.

Unfortunately, on the other hand, there are some horrible stories for those who didn't get to experience the amazing joy of love as they came into this world but instead endured hell on earth.

The enemy does not play fair. He will come for us while we're in the womb, out of the womb, and into the near future—setting the stage to ruin the destiny the Lord has planned for us since the foundation of the Earth. The enemy comes with a vengeance, seeking to corrupt our mindsets, even as small newborn babies. To destroy the purpose and plans in our lives before we even start growing into those beautiful young girls or mighty young men, by all the examples I gave above.

Sometimes—if not most of the time—this destruction is carried out by those who are supposed to love and care for us. I want to point out that these individuals have their own unresolved issues or hidden demons, and sometimes they are simply repeating a cycle that was placed upon them.

Regardless of the cause, they are now responsible for the damage inflicted upon the life they were meant to nurture.

As an infant or child, the precious little mind doesn't have the capability or understanding to comprehend these issues or demons—or to run for safety. This often leads many, as they grow up, to embark on a journey of searching for something they were created for from the very beginning: *Love.*

Whenever we lack what we were born to receive, we will be searching for it.

Our lives are not mistakes, even if we feel they are because of all the unanswered questions.

Leaving our lives as a blur from rejection, abuse, hardship, or any other unpleasant situation, we can forget the truth: *Your life isn't a mistake, no matter how deeply you convince yourself it is.*

You were carefully designed with a purpose.

We just have to work a little harder than those who were born to parents in healthy environments—parents who gave their children a head start.

Here's the reality: You don't have to count yourself out because you didn't receive those benefits.

We are not defined by what has been inflicted on us. Whatever that infliction looks like to you—it doesn't belong to you! It is not who you are!

It's simply what was placed upon you by the unhealthy influence of another.

Your identity is never in the hands of another—it took me a long time to understand that.

So, Psalm 139 does prove to be correct, even for the birth that was unwanted and for those for whom destruction was awaiting.

It was never your fault. Your birth was exciting, just like the next!

The Word says:

"You are fearfully and wonderfully made! His works are wonderful!"

Although the Lord has no control over the decisions of others because He gave us free will, His Word still stands true.

You were made with so much thought, love, and perfection—you were made to win.

There is nothing so damaging that the Lord cannot mend. You have every right to rewrite the script that was written for you and go from victim to victorious.

There are many children in the foster system, or with families that have handed them off to others, who feel unworthy—repeating phrases like, *"Something must be wrong with me, since my own mom didn't want me."*

But they never realize that those actions did not belong to them.

The truth is, it was never your issue—it was the decision of the individual who chose that path for their own reasons.

Although you might want an explanation for the actions that wounded you, will it really serve a purpose in your life?

You have the choice to love yourself, rewrite your script, and forgive (I will discuss forgiveness in a later chapter) the one who wrote it for you in the beginning.

Today, choose to believe in the beautiful gem that might be buried under those unhealthy memories.

Psalm 139 is you! You were born to win, and you have the victory in this life.

You deserved to be loved—maybe not by those who should have loved you (and that will be hard to swallow)—but I guarantee that if you focus on the One who gave you life, as spoken in the Scripture above, you won't have time to dwell on what you can't change.

Reflection Questions

1. The stories that you heard of your birth does it bring joy or sadness? Why ?
2. Do you believe the environment a baby is born into is crucial and why?
3. What do you believe are the best elements a baby needs ?
4. If you were birth into an unhealthy environment what can you do to change what happened to you ? Or if you were birth into a healthy environment what can your role be for someone who has not ?
5. Do you believe your life is valuable and precious why? Or why not ?

"Although my story began with a loving embrace, the joy of my birth soon gave way to challenges that would shape my early years. The innocence of childhood, so full of promise, was overshadowed by struggles that left me feeling lost and searching for answers."

Chapter 2

The Lost Child

Psalm 34:18

"The Lord is near to those who have a broken heart, and saves such as have a contrite spirit."

I had the beautiful privilege of working with children between the ages of 3 to 4 years for 25 years.

There is nothing more joyful than seeing a child being a child—intrigued by learning, exploring, free to be amazing little individuals, enjoying who they are in a big world.

As I would look at their beautiful smiles, in my mind, I would wonder and say a little prayer for those who might be enduring something we didn't see or were unaware of.

I was a child once, and I knew the burden of being trapped.

As a young girl, I would dream of being in a room with only white walls with a bunch of flashing-colored dots appearing and disappearing over each wall, sitting in the center of the room, realizing that there was no exit.

This was a reoccurring dream I had, that is still vivid to me as then. The only difference is that I understand today I was traumatized.

There are many children today whose lives have been changed drastically by someone who has made the decision to invade their innocence, awakening them to a realm a child should never, ever experience.

Unfortunately, we live in a world where so many innocent children are going to pay an undeserving price at the hands of a predator.

Leaving the young child's voice screaming:

- "I am only 3, 5, 7, 12 years old."

Shocked, confused, and lost, this young little boy or girl's soul has been crushed and broken—made accountable for the sins of those who should have loved and cared for them.

Screaming:

"I was just a young child who was brought into this world as an amazing gift. I had no blueprints. The only assignment was to help me be all that I can be in this life."

Your responsibility as a father, mother, family, friend, neighbor, or stranger was to care for someone lesser than you!

But instead, the precious gift has been misused in many capacities:

- Corrupted by words that poison.
- Hurt by hands that had no boundaries.
- Wounded by actions that lacked accountability.

Screaming:

- "My body parts were to be sacred until marriage."

- "The physical pain inflicted upon me was injustice at its worst."
- "The mental confusion and manipulation were wrong at every level."

Screaming:

"I am locked in captivity, burdened down from any childlike freedom. I was just a child trying to understand all that has come to disrupt my innocent life. I can hear the four walls, where I now reside, beating so loud: No Exit!"

Unable to understand that the individuals who take pleasure in hurting a fragile, innocent human being have been broken and crushed in some way also.

Like the little mouse thrown into an aquarium where a snake awaits, when the mouse finally realizes there is no way out, fear grips it because it knows it is going to be devoured.

It won't be long before the snake strikes the helpless little mouse.

What chance did it really have when it has been overpowered by something stronger than it?

No difference for a child who has now been trapped by someone stronger than them.

Leaving them traumatized and full of despair that will lead that child on a journey to pick up pieces they should have never been responsible for.

Screaming:

- "I am just a lost child."
- "Can anyone see me?"
- "Can anyone hear me?"

- "Does anyone care?"

Maybe these statements leave a blur in the mind or a sadness in the heart due to the blind eye and deaf ear. A wrenching in the soul that no one cared. Whatever the case, the word says:

"The Lord is near to those who have been broken and crushed in spirit."

To the lost child who is trapped,

To the inner child who isn't free,

To the child looking for answers and safety:

I want you to know there is still hope. There is someone looking, someone hearing, and someone who cares.

You might not understand it in your fragile, innocent state, but as you mature and realize, there is hope, and you don't have to live in captivity to an action you had no choice participating in.

There is hope to regain your strength, sanity, and power.

To live free from all that was inflicted on you.

There is hope in Jesus!

Reflection Questions

1. As a child, were you free or suppressed? Why or why not?
2. Is there an inner child still crying out for help? Why?
3. Is your inner child still led by any fear, anxiety, or panic from trauma?
4. Do you believe the inner child/adult can be healed from trauma? Why?

5. Do you believe there is hope to regain your strength, sanity, and power from horrible situations?

"As I navigated the confusion of my early years, the weight of my experiences left deep scars. The journey of feeling lost inevitably led to moments where I felt entirely broken, struggling to piece myself together."

Chapter 3:

Broken

Psalm 147:3

"He heals the brokenhearted, and binds up their wounds."

Childhood will frame the next journey that a young adolescent will take. If a child has been framed in the depth of abuse, there is a hole in the soul.

I want to tell you a story of a young girl named Crystal, who grew up in a home where there was mental, sexual, physical, and emotional abuse. This affected her whole being and soon thereafter became a breaking point.

Leaving her home as a 12-year-old girl, believing that there was something way better than what she was receiving at home, Crystal started a mission of searching for something she truly longed for: love and acceptance. But she soon found out that the streets were going to be just as vicious.

She was introduced to drugs, alcohol, men, and crime, and she found herself living in a way no young girl should ever experience in life. Lost and wounded, Crystal found herself sleeping in many places not fit for any human being, let alone a child.

She was like a frightened little cat looking for somewhere to hide for safety.

Here are just a few places she found refuge as she walked the streets with nowhere to go in those hours past midnight:

- Alone and cold, she climbed over a fence to get into a church where she would wrap herself inside a big tire to find rest.
- On another occasion, in the early morning hours, she climbed into the back of a truck, only to be awakened by someone yelling, *"Hey, what are you doing?"* Frightened, she jumped out and ran away, just like that frightened little cat.
- She met others like her, who helped her find shelter in an abandoned house, all the while wondering where she would go to get her next meal.

The streets kept her for years. All that was inflicted on her as a child was now being poured out in her adolescent years.

When a soul has been ripped apart, wounded, and filled with despair, there is a turmoil that takes place within. Crystal's soul needed mending due to the deep gashes she held within her core.

As she walked those streets, there were so many reminders of how she needed serious attention to those lacerations:

- Seeing a mother with her child.
- Hearing laughter from people going into a store.
- Sitting in front of a church while a service was going on, wearing clothes that had not been changed in a day or two.

She often pondered:

- "Am I just invisible to everyone?"
- "Does anyone see the gashes that are bleeding and spilling out everywhere?"
- "Does anyone even realize I am just 12, 13, or 14 years old?"

She wondered if anyone had the compassion to look into the windows of her soul and see how hollow she was. She longed to be genuinely loved, hugged, and cared for—or maybe just to hear a whisper: *"It's going to be okay."*

Instead, she asked herself if she was just another runaway statistic, dismissed as an unruly, rebellious teenager.

A Harsh Reality

There are many young boys and girls on the streets wandering roads that lead nowhere. They are unnoticed, unheard, and taken advantage of by many.

Statistics show that there are 1 to 3 million runaway and homeless kids living on the streets in the United States *(kidshealth.org)*.

Psalm 147:3 says, *"He heals the brokenhearted."*

Crystal's heart is a perfect example of one crushed beyond repair in some eyes. She was considered "damaged goods." Who would want her around, especially near their children? When someone looks unrepairable, they are seen as a threat.

That same scripture says, *"He binds up their wounds."* Her wounds were very deep from the years of abuse she endured. If a wound is not healed properly, it will get reinfected. When wounds are really deep, healing takes time—a process that requires placing yourself in the right environment to receive divine healing.

Hope for the Broken

Crystal's life represents the many young people on the streets today:

- Caught up in drugs.
- Running wild.
- Experiencing things that devalue their lives.

There are also adults living in their past traumas who have not been freed from the memories that still haunt them. Their inner child is still screaming for help, as though the abuse and trauma are still happening.

No matter where you are, you are not alone. There are many who understand the lonely walk of rejection, hurt, anger, confusion, and stigma.

Do not carry something that was never yours to carry. It's time to dismantle that place of pain.

- It was never intended for you from the beginning.
- It's time to embrace healing.
- It's time to heal the wounds.
- It's time to be free and move on.

There is so much waiting for you:

- Life abundant.
- Healing and restoration.

No matter how deep your gashes are, they are not unnoticed, and they can be mended. Breathe. Give yourself what you righteously deserve: a second chance.

Jesus can heal a broken heart and mend a wound. You deserve the beautiful life He has destined for you. Reach for it, take it, and run. There is life in the midst of the darkest places.

Reflection Questions

1. Who molded your upbringing? Was it healthy or unhealthy guidance?
2. As a young teen, have you ever felt alone? Why or why not?
3. Did you feel unseen or unheard? Why or why not?
4. When dealing with unpleasant and hurtful situations, did it lead you to a destructive path?
5. Do you believe that no matter how crushed, damaged, or broken someone is, they can be repaired? Why or why not?

"In my brokenness, I sought solace in paths that seemed to offer escape but instead led me further from healing. The choices I made during this time often took me down the wrong road, with consequences that echoed throughout my life."

Chapter 4

Wrong Road

Proverbs 14:12

There is a way that seems right to a man, but its end is the way of death.

There where many many roads i choose from in life and many of them seemed right til i realize the destruction that was awaiting.

I mentioned in a previous chapter that crystal went to the streets where she thought it would be better from the abuse she endured in the four walls of her home. When she soon found out it was an absolute delusion and she was sinking rapidly into a darker hole.

Time will reveal whether or not the paths we have chosen were right even if we in our own logic believed they were.

I want us to know this will pertain to every facet of life.

The paths I took were differently unwise and heartbreaking and very costly to my well-being.

If those paths didn't add to my life, they were stripping away at the very essence of who I was intended to be.

Every road that leads to destruction no matter the capacity will never have any good thing to offer and each road truly brings death in so many ways.

Meaning there is no prosperity, substance, elevation there and it will be a dead barren land with No fruitfulness!

Our lives are gift to achieve so much in this world and all it has to offer. Yet if we make one wrong turn it can be destroyed by the darkness of those places, we made a decision to walk in.

Which will eventually kill our self worth, value, self esteem or any chance of a solid education that will bring an empowered life.

I understood that every path I took on those streets killed the very essence of my worth, value, self-esteem and education I could receive.

I want to elaborate on these 4 for just a little bit.

I. Self Worth

Self worth, is the feeling you have good qualities and have achieved good things.

(Collins Dictionary)

Every single person on this earth is a gift who has the ability to give back into this world with there amazing qualities and all the great things they have achieved. If The qualities are tainted by whatever hardship someone has endured in life it can eventually lead them down a destructive path that strangles and suppress the worth of an individual, society can add to this by their perception of those who have lost their way, which can be understandable because the exterior of such a person is saying loud and clear criminal, drug addict, alcoholic promiscuous, unruly, prostitute, BEWARE.

When someone can only see the destructive pattern of an individual, they will never be able to understand the root of the outward appearance.

The inward parts of an individual is saying hurt, used, abused, damaged, broken, divorced, rejected, rage HELP ME!

I do want to point out that someone's perception of you in a struggling season might have some truth, but it's not the whole truth.

For instance, someone might see a homeless person but never realizing that the true individual is bounded inside.

Held by all the horrible experiences, losses, let downs, disappointments that lead them to such a place of defeat.

Do you know that research shows that 31% to 46% of youth exiting foster care experience homelessness by age 26.

(foster care statistics)

It will take someone very special to help an individual see what really resides deep within. When they have succumbed to a place like those in foster care.

The word says, in Isaiah 61:3 he gave Israel beauty for ashes. Israel was in a fallen state and God Almighty was restoring them back to their rightful place.

Basically, Israel took a wrong turn that brought them to a devastating outcome but the Lord promises them beauty for all the ashes.

We must remember Beauty can always be pulled out of every bad or wrong choice.

I want us to just take a moment just to close your eyes and look deep deep inside, beneath all the ashes and search for the beauty!

The beauty you don't believe is there.

The beauty you thought was gone.

The beauty you believe can't be found! Come on Keep searching!

People don't just lose their self-worth. It's taken by the ashes.

II. Value

Consider (someone or something) to be important or beneficial; have a high opinion of.

(Oxford Dictionary)

The decisions we make are truly based on how much we value ourselves weather knowing or unknowing.

For instance, a woman that finds herself in a relationship that destroys her to the point where she can't even hold her head up high, stripped from all her self esteem by the toxic behavior bestowed upon her.

Subjected to an individual who is controlling, obsessive and an abusive partner.

Lost in a relationship that was supposed to be precious and full of adventure as they have come together as one. But soon finds out the relationship doesn't bring any security or love.

She is now fueled by the physical pain and words that have slashed her very being is now in a place where She can barely recognize herself, forgetting the beautiful diamond that she was created to be. although there have been many anticipating times to run or hearing the small voice that says get out!

She still is unable to find the courage or strength to leave, paralyzed by the words and the fear, the intense uncertainty has crippled her.

Confused, humiliated and shamed by the division of love and hate and for allowing someone to devalue her.

The word says in James 1:17 every good gift, and every perfect gift is from above. (NKJV).

Your life is a gift and if you have ever received a gift there is so much joy and excitement as you are getting ready to carefully unwrap it.

We are no different. We need to be very careful how we handle and place our special gift of life.

Never placing it somewhere it will be devalued, unappreciated or taken for granted.

You owe to yourself to take care of the precious gift that was given to you from above. There is a cemetery full of amazing parents, brilliant teenagers, doctors, lawyers, teachers, writers and so much more who didn't value the gift.

Today, make a decision to value your gift.

III. Low Self Esteem

When someone lacks confidence of who they are and what they can do.

(Web MD)

A place of how we value and perceive ourselves.

When we don't have the right perception about ourselves, we will allow anything because we don't see anything good within.

This is a very dangerous place because it can allow others to dictate our lives.

I want to share an experience of something I witnessed on the streets of south central.

There was a young girl same age 13 years old.

The older women who were prostituting on the streets took hold of her and misused her in so many ways.

Although I was on those streets doing bad myself in many different ways.

I still remember my thoughts unable to comprehend why she would let them do so many degrading things to her.

I didn't understand then that her belief in herself as well as mine was so off.

When someone has no self-worth or value, they believe they only deserve the bottom of that barrel.

I am sure the sound rang deep and loud in her as it did me. The screeching sound that said "I'm not good enough", that killed every ambition to even want to try to get out believing I deserve this!

Defeated by our own thoughts and words that come to torment my mind, followed by a body language yelling no Confidence!

The word of God say in proverbs 23:7 For as he thinks in his heart, so is he ."

Eat and drink.!" he says to you,

But His heart is not with you. (NKJV).

Our actions, behavior, language will show how we think about ourselves and

What we think about ourselves is more crucial than what others think of us.

I understand this can be challenging for the one who had negative hurtful words and behavior drilled into their mind.

But ... Here a news flash! you have the power to use the delete button to every single voice that comes to condemn you in any way and in return replace it with the voice coming from the powerful word of God.

You are free (2 Corinthians 3:17)

You are loved (John 3:16)

You are blessed (Jeremiah 17:7)

You are a conquer (Romans 8:37)

You are victorious (Philippians 4:13) (NKJV).

There are many more powerful scriptures that have been given to and for you,

Free of charge. Absolutely no cost, but for you only to Believe.

IV. Education

The act or process of imparting or acquiring general

knowledge, developing the powers of reasoning and judgment, and generally of preparing oneself or others intellectually for a mature life. (Dictionary.com)

When the mind and body are not healthy the desire to be learned in any healthy way is gone.

The passion you are fueled by is what leads a person.

For instance, those that care for their future follows all the necessary steps to become something productive in society. Taking every opportunity seriously, achieving the grades to make it possible followed by parents and family who will applause them on every effort.

Someone once told me in order to be great you must sit with the great. Be taught by the great. Learn from the great.

Always staying teachable. In this case the great being Jesus Christ first, then followed by great men and women who will have life changing impact on our lives. Those who are truly heaven sent.

But what happens to the one who has been counted out because of the cards that have been dealt to them in life by any traumatic lifestyle which has led to layers on top of layers of destructive behavior.

When the passion is fueled by the total opposite of the one striving to be the best.

There are two resilient hearts here, the first heart has been given every chance possible with encouragement, the right guidance and tools to accomplish all they need to conquer in life.

The second heart has been torn down and hardened by the things that have weighed them down in life.

Which makes everything seem so impossible.

Unable to realize that one stepping stone will lead to another and it is truly no different from a downward spiral effect.

It will take a perfect love, wisdom and understanding to help anyone who has lost hope. Your participation is to place your feet on the first stepping stones.

The mind is so powerful! And it is ready to live and learn. I have seen many lives turned around. Removing themselves from everything destroying them, getting educated and walking into their purpose with the faith in Jesus Christ as he guides them.

For those also dealing with the second heart it is not your final destination. The word of God in Isaiah 40:31 says:

But those who wait on the LORD shall renew their strength; They shall mount up with wings like eagles, they shall run and not be weary, they shall walk and not faint. (NKJV).

I want to share with you a beautiful story on the eagle renewed strength. (medium.com)

Eagles, get or grow stronger with age, whilst humans get or grow weaker with age. This is because the Eagles have a restoration or renewal process in their mid 40's. The eagle goes through a painful process for 5 months as part of this restoration. The process requires that the eagle fly to a mountaintop and sit on its nest. There the eagle Knocks its beak against a rock until it plucks it out. Then the eagle will wait for a new beak to grow back, and then it will pluck out its talons. When is new talons grow back, the eagle starts plucking its old, aged feathers. The eagle will then wait for the new feathers to grow, and once it grows, the eagle takes its famous, flight of rebirth and lives for 30 more years. The Eagle will regain, vigor, renew its strength, live longer, and soar higher.

I love how the Lord uses his creation to get his scripture across to us. The eagle process lets us see that getting rid of the old to gain and renew our strength is always going to be painful but as we go through this process and release all that has hindered our growth because of all the wrong roads one has walked on we are like the eagle being rebirth. It will never be easy letting go of our past because it will always cost us something but as we do watch out! we are ready to soar.

Soar eagle you were meant to fly.

Reflection Questions

1. Do you believe time reveals everything? Why or why not ?
2. Do you believe the roads you choose can lead to destruction Why ?
3. Can anything that has brought destruction be turned into triumph?
4. Are you able to soar like an eagle after some devastating choices ? Why or why not ?
5. Do you believe your life is a gift and has a purpose in this world ? Why or why not ?

"Even amidst the missteps and wrong turns, glimmers of hope began to break through. It was in these moments of despair that I witnessed miracles that reminded me of the possibilities for redemption."

Chapter 5

The Miracle

Psalm 127: 3

Behold, children are a heritage from the Lord, the fruit of the womb is a reward.

The second part to this verse says the fruit of the womb is a reward. Reward meaning the beautiful miracle of being able to conceive a child.

There will be those who will see the reward and treasure it.

Those who will take that reward for granted.

Those who will not appreciate the reward.

Those who will bare no reward for many reasons.

In the United States 10% of women from age 15-44 have difficulty getting pregnant or staying pregnant.

(CDC)

There is a deep void for a barren woman who has a desire to have children but cannot this remind me of a story in the Bible of a woman named Hannah in

1 Samuel chapter 1 who understood that void. The word of God said she was in bitterness of soul and wept sore from the longing of wanting a child.

She continually came before God in desperation praying for him to bless her womb.

Hannah knew first hand how it felt to be barren and desire something she could not obtain.

This is a reality for many women today who would love to have this opportunity of motherhood. The opportunity to bring another living being into this world enjoying every moment of holding a precious little life in their arms as they gaze into those tiny eyes. Who wouldn't want to experience this miraculous gift.

Motherhood is so beautiful especially when you're ready for it.

I was granted the gift of being a mom.

At the age of 16, which was a baby having a baby.

A baby will always be a gift!

But the decisions outside of planning and being ready for this precious little miracle can be devastating and hard on the baby if you are not ready.

Before I go on,

I truly encourage you to prepare with your significant other to make sure you are both ready to care for such a great responsibility.

Especially for the wellbeing of the baby.

I truly didn't even understand what I got myself into and all the mix emotions I was going through.

I was in no position to bring an innocent precious little human being into this world in the condition I was in which was so unfair to my daughter and eventually the other 3 that would follow.

For those who have birth a child without preparation. You still have an amazing opportunity to make a turnaround.

But for those who know their lives are in no position to bring a child into this world because the lifestyle they are in are very unhealthy and unstable. This is a moment of transparency for you and to make a life changing decision for yourself first that you may be healthy for your children, then taking all the positive healthy steps to guide your children to a new path.

The word of God says in Romans 8:28,

And we know that all things work together for good to those who love God, to those who are called according to his purpose (NKJV).

I spoke about birth in chapter 1,

How babies are born into healthy or unhealthy families Never realizing that my life would one day reflect the very thing I endured and hated with a passion just at a different degree.

One thing I have come to see is no matter what degree of abuse a child endures for instance neglect, emotional, mental, physical or sexual the child is never going to sit there and weigh the balances.

No! The Pain and void are the reality. What has been inflicted on them is just as real as the next.

So, although it wasn't the same kind abuse. It was abuse!

And I would one day realize and have to live with this brutal truth.

Questioning myself "what have I done! "

By Birthing a beautiful baby into an environment that was reckless unstable and very unhealthy.

Living so carelessly, feeding my body with uncontrolled substances (drugs and alcohol) never taking into consideration I was not just destroying myself but a beautiful living being within me,

I put myself into so many compromising situations that could and did have a great effect on the innocent life now growing inside me.

Unteachable to the knowledge that each trimester had a great importance in so many detrimental ways.

Never trying to understand the depths of each action I was taking.

No consideration for my wellbeing or the precious gift growing inside.

But how could I see,

If I was unable to get past the memories that still haunted me!

How could I see,

If my thoughts were governed by the injustice, mistreatment that consumed me!

How could I see, if my misery drowned my soul!

How could I see, if I had no intention of changing my pattern!

How could I see, if I entertained my own pity party!

How could I see, if I was so self absorbed!

I was called to be a parent, but yet I was so far from it.

Unable to produce that which I felt was deprived from my own life.

Unable to fulfill a role that was not molded for me.

"How will I love her"?

If love has been distorted to me!

"How will I care"

If I don't even care for myself!

"How will I protect her"

If I never felt protected!

"Where will I lead her"

If I don't even know where I'm going!

There is story in the book of Ruth of a woman named Naomi.

(I want to just paraphrase this story in Ruth chapters 1-4 (NKJV).

Naomi left her land with her husband and two sons and went to a foreign land called Moab.

Soon after she faces some devastating occurrences, her husband passes away then her two sons.

The grief of losing her whole family lead her back home to Judah.

One can only imagine how Naomi felt going back stripped from all that she loved.

Devastated, broken, shocked, lost.

The word says in Ruth 1:19-20

That the people were stirred saying

"Can this be Naomi"?

Naomi responded "don't Call me Naomi, call me Mara "which means the Lord has dealt bitterly with my life.

There will differently be some situations that will leave us bitter. Here Naomi has been stripped from all she loved and known. This story stands true for every child, every person who lives with the inner child that has been violated, stripped in some capacity.

This story has a beautiful ending proving how we start is not the final answer. The Seasons in life that can make us bitter is only an opportunity for us to see how great God is!

His restoration healing power is as real for us now as it was for Naomi then.

If you ever find yourself in a bitter, stripped season understand that is exactly what it is, a SEASON!

It can change for you just like it did for Naomi she was Restored but not alone, her daughter in law Ruth also was given a second chance.

Meaning restoration will not just affect you but others around you! The word of God say in Acts 16:31, So they said, "Believe on the Lord Jesus Christ, and you will be saved, you and your household." (NKJV).

I can testify to this beautiful passage and scripture in the Bible because I have witnessed it with my own eyes.

My beautiful baby I gave birth too along with my 3 other amazing daughters who Are a true reflection of how we started did not determine their future. Me being a teen mom was only part of my story.

Statistics show that in 2020 the birth rate to teens from age 15-19 yrs old was 15.4 % here in the US and 91.7% were born outside of marriage and This does not include those babies who were born to parents who dealt with addictions.

(HHS Office of Population Affairs)

There are many out there today who are walking in my shoes, and there are many teens who didn't how I applaud you! My heart rejoices to know some will not have to experience roads that only bring destruction.

To those who did take wrong roads it not over I have seen the miracles! I am a living witness to them flourishing into beautiful women and you would not even believe for one minute they had been born to a mother who was considered unlikely to succeed or them. You see God grace is not there for us to continue in wrong paths, his grace is there to help through the journey so we come out shinning from anything that is destroying us.

2 Corinthians 12:9 says,

And he said to me, "My grace is sufficient for you, for My strength is made perfect in weakness. "Therefore, most gladly I will rather boast in my infirmities, that the power of Christ rest upon me. (NKJV).

Be encouraged today the possibilities that come from a mighty God will amaze you!

The word of God says in Luke 18:27

But he said, "The things which are impossible with men are possible with God." (NKJV).

If you are the woman who cannot bare the reward for whatever reason there is hope!

Or the woman who took the precious reward for granted or didn't appreciate, treasure it like I spoke about in the beginning of this chapter there is HOPE!

There is always hope!

Reflection Questions

1. Is motherhood a privilege?
2. What is your responsibility as you become a mother ?
3. Is it important to prepare before choosing to bring a little life into this world? Why ?
4. If you are unhealed do you believe this will have an impact on motherhood?
5. Do you believe if you failed as a mom things can be turned around? Why or why not ?

"While the miracle of new beginnings inspired hope, I could not escape the guilt that lingered from past actions and choices. This guilt weighed heavily on me, becoming a burden I needed to confront."

Chapter 6

Guilty

Proverbs 21:8

The way of the guilty man is perverse; But as for the pure, his work is right.

Guilty means justly chargeable with a particular fault or error.

Perverse means a deviation from righteousness and a turning away from the true intent or purpose.

(Webster dictionary)

When someone is found guilty in court it means the crime they committed has been found to be true and now the penalty must be paid.

Depending on the crime and its severity they will pay usually by jail, fines or probation.

This guilty verdict is based on the perverse ways the individual has taken.

This is a heavy p but definitely isn't unrepairable.

As long as someone doesn't get stuck in the guilt, or a hardened heart.

Everyone in this life time will be guilty of something they could not change and depending on the severity it will determine the struggle of letting it go.

If the individual can't let it go it will be a

Resounding echo.

Repeating words like "you just couldn't Accomplish the standard, education, task"!

"You miss the mark of what you where accountable and responsible for"!

"You just down right failed"!

Whatever the case, now you have to live with the regrets. Realizing there nothing else you can do about it because the action has already taken place.

It becomes worse when the action just doesn't affect you, but also those around you.

Guilt will have you living in a place trying to pay a price that you can never repay.

For instance, if someone has failed at being a parent in a serve way like I mentioned in the previous chapter.

They can become consumed with guilt always trying to make up for a debt they truly can't repay because that child or children who have now come to ages of accountability must endure their own healing process. Your participation can be positive if they are ready to hear you acknowledge your faults and are willing to apologize for those devastating errors. This goes for any relationship that is damaged.

It very necessary to evaluate if this is coming from a well place so that you are not crucifying yourself over and over for the errors you can't change that are secretly killing you internally.

You must let go so that you are in complete wholeness to be effectual for those who have been affected by the errors on their life.

Guilt is a negative emotion that relates to feelings bad about a certain behavior or action. (Connecte)

Unfortunately, it does not stop with just the negative emotions but guilt may eventually affect one self esteem and self worth, and can lead to maladaptive behaviors that end up harming you. (quoted by Dr. Ho)

So, someone who can't change what they have done from the negative actions they placed on others can become self-destructive.

This can be accompanied by filling the guilt, self condemnation with alcohol, drugs or the maladaptive behaviors.

(Maladaptive behavior is like someone who oversleeps because of their depression.)

All these are indicators that an individual is avoiding the truth because it to painful to confront.

Once again, we all will fail or fall short at something, but the key is getting up no matter how damaging or ugly that truth is. we must tackle it head on.

In my journey of life, I have gathered all 4 of my daughters to apologize to them for falling short of a mother and the hardship I have caused them.

I have done this several times to the point where they have told me to stop!

Til this day every time I have a pivotal moment of how wonderful the Lord has spared them and keep them.

I find another chance to validate my beautiful daughters.

Reminding them it was never them.

I was the responsible party for what i did or did not do without excuse.

How proud I am of them and the mothers they are to their children. You see time will always reveal truth. And when we made wrong choices and truth stares us straight in the face it will be a hard pill to swallow until you see the beauty of what God has done!

I want to give you two examples.

My first one is the one I just described there was a time I would have to look at my daughters and see the beautiful mothers they were to their children making sure every need of is meet for their little ones mentally, emotionally, physically, education, sports plus more. There was a time I sat there beating myself up because I didn't give them what they needed most! A mother and that truth was speaking so loud and clear as I had to look into their lives and realize every where I fell short.

Luke 22:34,54-62, Gives a detailed story of a man falling short to someone he loved and having to face the harsh truth of letting someone he loved down.

In Luke 22:34 it says, then he said, "I tell you Peter, the rooster shall not crow this day before you will deny three times that you know me." (NKJV).

Jesus is preparing for his journey to the cross and he letting his disciple Peter know , you are going to deny me three times in the scripture above this one Peter is proclaiming is undying devotion to Jesus but as you read through 54-62 you see the frailty of man and how someone can have the best intentions, scream their unending devotion as Peter did but in verses 61-62 it says, And the Lord turned and looked at Peter. Then Peter remembered the word of the Lord how he said to him, "Before the rooster crows, you will deny Me three times." So, Peter went out and wept bitterly. (NKJV).

How I love this story it allows me to see that I am not the only one who will have to face the truth of not living up to what I have said or what I was responsible for to those I loved and once again what a price to pay even for Peter he went out and wept bitterly for falling short to the one he ate with, lived with, who discipled him and loved him dearly.

My second example of that brutal truth is when I was attending a church service, they presented a drama play, in this drama the women were playing a scene of two mothers who were drinking getting all dolled up to venture out into the night life. The women portrayed this as a reoccurring pattern.

They feed their kids put them to bed so they could hurry up and leave yet there was no supervision.

Their unhealthy desires were more important than the children.

I remember tears were just falling from my eyes, uncontrollable tears that rolled and kept rolling.

And it wasn't because I was consumed with guilt anymore or the regret that use burned in my soul that repeated "If I could just have one more chance to do it all over again."

The tears were from a place of understanding where I was once at, undeniably knowing the skit was me. When we are blind and lost there no revelation but something beautiful happens when the light turns on and you can see. You know where you're at and are able to get up and move forward.

I knew I didn't live there anymore I use to be the women in the skit. How grateful I was to see how far I had came walking in the direction continually of who I was really meant to be, in this case a mother.

There was so much changing power in watching my daughter's groom their children and the drama play for me.

The tears will always be different for me now!

These tears no longer captivate me to a place that bounds me like my first example.

We do get second, third and sometimes more chances to get it right. And when you do the gratefulness and thankfulness that will flood your soul knowing you were released from a debt you couldn't pay will leave you speechless.

I was given another chance to be the best version of myself so I can be well for my children, grandchildren, family and this can only be done by the only one who has the power to change the heart of man, Jesus!

Another chance to show others with the grace of God anything is achievable When you acknowledge those errors and have true remorse for our actions.

Willing to forgive yourself and receiving the precious forgiveness of God.

We are not disqualified by all the ugliness we can allow when we become honest to ourselves that we made mistakes, hurt the ones we were to care and love.

This place brings so much appreciation to the only one who can set us free. Jesus!

The word says in psalm 139:23-24

Search me, O God, and know my heart! Try me and know my thoughts!

And see if there be any grievous way in me, and lead me in the way everlasting.

This is such a beautiful scripture not to be viewed in a negative manner.

A scripture of coming once again to the truth of what is really residing in us so we may no longer carry anything that does not benefit us. Removing ourselves from a perverse way into a correct path. In doing this the Lord restores everything to its proper order.

The word also says in Romans 8:1

Therefore, there is now no condemnation for those who are in Christ Jesus.

Commendation will also kill the very essence of who you were created to be.

By magnifying how guilty you are!

Sounding Repeatedly "you are unworthy and definitely very undeserving "!

Stop!

Just listen to the voice that has come to haunt you like a scratch record that just continues to repeat itself over and over.

Recognize the voice is it yours or someone else's that keeps you drowning.

What voice fuels your failures reminding you that you failed as a husband, wife , child, boss, home owner, career, job , five fold minster or elsewhere.

What voice is keeping you?

Recognize it! run from it!

Because It will never let you rest.

Now hold on to the peace that was freely given to you and be the best version you were created to be.

Reflection Questions

1. What effects can guilt have on your life?
2. Can guilt harden someone heart?
3. Do you believe that you deserve to keep punishing yourself for something you can't change?
4. What failures haunt you with regrets?
5. Do you believe you can obtain peace over things you cannot change ?

"Carrying guilt often goes hand in hand with the challenge of forgiveness. As I struggled to forgive myself, I realized that letting go of anger toward others was equally essential for my healing."

Chapter 7

Unforgiving

Mathew 6:14-15

For if you forgive men Their trespasses, your heavenly father will also forgive you. But if you do not forgive men their trespasses, neither will your father forgive your trespasses.

This scripture can be so challenging especially for the one who has endured mistreatment at its worst. Who really wants to forgive someone that has hurt them I know I didn't. Sounds insane right?

Horrifying stories that can leave anyone wondering how did they get through it all. Those stories that are not only hard to put in words but cringing unbelievable.

There are just some things in life that are very difficult to pardon period, but forgiveness doesn't have anything to do with the other person and forgiveness doesn't mean you stay around an individual that continues to abuse you in any form.

I once read Forgiveness means you accept what wrongs have been done to you, you let go of those wrongs, you calm your heart with God's love and patience, and you begin again with or without that person, it's up to you.

(Thought catalog.com)

It is also Very important not to allow any kind of pressure on you to be forgiving this is a decision that needs to be a solid conscious conclusion from the depths of your heart.

Don't allow some to assume you don't forgive because you choose not to be around an individual who destroyed your life in some capacity. It's absolutely ok to stay in the place you feel safe until the next step comes.

In life I have come to see that it was very difficult for me to forgive the person who took advantage of my innocence and vulnerability because they knew they could.

How could I ever fight back anyways when I was too young to understand the manipulation intimidation, and all the controlling behavior that was being feed to me by the individual who was grooming me in deception.

Not to mention a predator looks like a giant to any child little eyes. Until the fear is gone and resentment and hate steps in.

There will soon come an age where any child who is being abused will rebel and resist any deception that was keeping them bound by Fear.

At least that was my experience those words penetrating my soul were like an alarm that rang so loud screaming

"I will never let anyone hurt me again!"

The unforgiveness one day fueled into rage, anger, hate. I was Going from being controlled to uncontrollable really quick with no stop button.

I no longer viewed the giant who I was terrified of as undefeatable but now as an enemy! A person who represented evil to me and had no good intentions for me other than keeping me trapped by deception to misuse my fragile life.

Something happens to a child who starts realizing all homes are not the same. And the dark secrets that lingered in their home have now been exposed by the measuring of a healthy home and the child is now comprehending not every family is the same and those dark secrets were very abnormal and unjust.

They become aware and that awareness will bring embarrassment, humiliation, the dread of How could I ever tell this disturbing secret to anyone.

It's my fault,

This place consumed me for years. The accountability that I placed on myself, the responsibility I accepted to what was happening to me was horrible to say at the least.

Everyone has a limit and mine was at the age of 12 years. It's still unbelievable to me how I found the courage to get out at that age sadly not to a safe place.

I learned really quick my unforgiveness was more for my mom than the one that hurt me. Never understanding why, she gave him so much authority over me when he wasn't even my biological father. (Please understand that I do know there are many amazing step- fathers and many biological fathers that hurt their own children in drastic ways.)

The anger that fueled me in my younger age could not grasp why? Why? Why?

Didn't you watch out for me as my mom?

How did you allow him to gain so much control over my life?

Couldn't you see the man he really was?

Why did you abandon me as a mom

I had so many unanswered questions for my mom and Although I had so much ill feelings for the real perpetrator.

I still held my mom very much accountable. Every time I had an opportunity, I held her to the stake with my hurtful words of hatred spilling from my soul. (A stake is a wooden post with a point in the end so it can be driven into the ground, Unmovable they would tie a person on there to burn them as a punishment.)

Meaning I use this metaphor of how I held my mother tied down to every single thing I experienced in my childhood , it was her fault in my eyes all that I went through and her inability to care and protect me was intensified at it's greatest and i wanted her to know what a horrible mother human being she was to me and I did by never letting her rest from my punishment because I felt she was worse than the person who was truly hurting me.

I wanted her to hear and feel all the pain I was going through and had gone through maybe I really believed it would bring some kind satisfaction to me but it didn't.

I know to some who reads this might believe my actions were justifiable for all I endured as a kid under my mom care.

How I understand, because so did I at that point of my life when I was led by all my damaging emotions that I had the right to feel because no little child deserves any kind of abuse what wasn't rightful was letting those damaging emotions rule my life for many years to come.

There came a time in my life when the memory came back to me the night, I told my mom what we had been going with her husband. I'll never forget how she cried. It was a wailing as though someone had died a painful horrible cry. Not to mention she attacked him this memory was the beginning of my breakthrough for my life that would eventually flow into both of our lives.

I started looking at my mom with different eyes. Eyes that seen a victim but just at a different capacity.

And all the junk I carried for years eventually started slowly dissipating. And in due time the love for my mom came back.

You see my mom gave her life to Christ when I turned 12 because she couldn't understand what I was going through in the beginning and it was killing her to see there was nothing she could do.

The mother that I felt let me down in so many ways would be the same mother who would pray for my deliverance for years and years to come, this is why I'm writing this book today the word say in James 5:16

Therefore, confess your sins to each other and pray for each other so that you may be healed. The prayer of the righteous person is powerful and effective.

We can never change the past or dwell there but we do have the awesome ability to change our future! The Lord truly shines brightest in dark places and situations.

The Lord allowed my mom to see me delivered from all junk that kept my mind heart and soul.

The word says in proverbs 17:9

Love prospers when a fault is forgiven, but dwelling on it separates close friend.

So, if it has the power to separate close friends can u imagine within a family. When we allow forgiveness to reign love can restore the hardest situations in life.

We all know Rome wasn't built in a day! It was a long journey for me and my mom but when I tell you God restored our relationship. He restored it!

My mom is my best friend today and my prayer partner, the one who holds us together today by her strong belief in the Lord word and the faith she exhibits

She has witnessed his goodness upon my life along with my sister who endured so much also.

I'm blessed to call her my mom today.

I have learned and will not give one ounce of attention to the past that held me down with all its misery.

Forgiveness was a major part of our healing. When I asked her if it was ok to write this chapter she said "yes, you write the truth I believe it will set many free."

Somebody might be thinking what about the one who violated you? I can understand that but he wasn't my blood relative. He was someone who took advantage of a woman with two beautiful girls in my eyes. Family is always harder for me and is very personal.

Please don't misunderstand me. I had so much hatred and anger for him also.

But when I realized the power of forgiveness, how I had the power to not allow him to imprison me in my own mind or keep me sitting in a room with no exit. I finally realized that person couldn't hurt me no more or keep me trapped no longer. I was free. We can't allow individuals to imprison our mind. The energy one can put into all that they did to you will leave you lifeless. You have the power to release them and move forward.

Has anyone trapped you today with unforgiveness?

Don't get stuck in believing you are letting them get away with what they have done.

That's a lie! You are taking your life back.

Release them from your mind, heart, and soul.

I want to mention my perpetrator did reach out to me telling me he hopes I can find it in my heart to forgive him. ITHOGM was a very challenging time because the past wants to creep back in. We have to be determined to not go back so

My response was I forgave you a long time ago. I pray you find your peace with God.

My heart harbors no ill thoughts for him.

May he one day realize all he has done to two innocent girls and how it really damages the innocence of that life if he hasn't already.

But nevertheless we all will have to look in the mirror and face who we really are and that we can't get away from. Choose to be free from all that tries to trap you.

I purposely live on purpose the Lord has given me complete freedom and I take hold of it and enjoy every moment I have here on earth.

The word says in Jhon 8:36 so if the son sets you free, you will be free indeed.

You were not created to be kept tormented by the thoughts that can haunt you till the very life is drained out of you, or the heart that is bleeding by those memories that can cripple you, or the anguish that can bring turmoil in the soul because of the unforgiveness.

You have the power to be free with one decision: to release everyone and anyone who has been imprisoned in your mind.

You can be free!

It only takes three words:

I forgive _____.

Reflection Questions

1. Is forgiving someone hard for you?
2. When you forgive the one who hurt you is it for you or them? Why?
3. Does forgiving make you feel they got away with it?
4. Does forgiveness mean you have to be around the person?
5. Does forgiveness set you free?

"The journey toward forgiveness opened the door to a greater truth: peace cannot coexist with chaos. It was only when I sought God wholeheartedly that I began to understand the true meaning of peace."

Chapter 8

Where there is no peace, there is no God

Isaiah 26:3

You will keep him in perfect peace, whose mind is stayed on You, because he trusts in you.

I know you might understand by now that I have given you a portion of my story and all the storms that I have endured.

Storms that were inflicted upon me, and that I inflicted upon myself!

Nevertheless, many of them have left me gasping for air. Realizing the chaos and confusion is what led to my life being consumed by all those things I spoke about in the previous chapters that continued to rehearse in my mind over and over Again for many years. Never realizing that my life was in shambles and my soul was very uneasy and very restless.

I came to understand that any kind of tranquility was taken from me the day my life was interrupted by someone else's demons leaving me agitated, anxious, disturbed at a very young age unable to realize what true serenity really was because I only tasted of the unhealthy environment. Here I'm talking about my childhood but there are marriages, relationships of different kinds, finances that face some alarming situations that can really come in and leave you consumed.

There is a divine peace the Lord wants to give us in the midst of our difficulties whether they are great or small, worrisome or traumatic, a peace that surpasses all understanding. A peace not understandable to man unless they have met the prince of peace who is Jesus.

Isaiah 9:6 says, for to us a child is born, to us a son is given, and the government will be on his shoulders. And he will be called Wonderful Counselor, Mighty God, Everlasting Father, PRINCE OF PEACE. Jesus was born so that we may have access to many beautiful benefits and peace is one! A peace that is able to consume us beyond any human efforts.

A calmness that is given within as we trust the Lord in the most challenging situations, deepest anguish, troubling experiences especially when we know we don't have no control over them. I want to assure you that it will take time to learn how to master staying in a place of serenity.

Psalm 4:8 says,

I will both lie down in peace and sleep; For you alone, O Lord, make me dwell in safety. (NKJV).

I want to give you an example of this In Matthew 8:23-25 the word says,

Now when he got into a boat, His disciples followed Him.

And suddenly a great tempest arose on the sea, so that the boat was covered with waves. But He was asleep.

Then His disciples came to Him and awoke Him, saying, "Lord, save us! We are perishing!" (NKJV).

The disciples found themselves in a place where there was no time to think about it, prepare for it, they had been hit with a suddenly situation at its greatest!

Leaving them vulnerable and overtaken by what was before them.

We are No different when something has overtaken us and consumed us leaving our minds tormented by the terrible blows that hit our lives.

The boat symbolizes how we can be rocked to and fro by the issue of life, the wind and sea are all the trails and tribulations that can impact our lives and how freighting they can be.

Jesus' whole desire is for us to cling to his peace as the boat rocks and as the waves are over taking us, giving us a place of stillness as the winds blow.

Jesus wants us to experience a tranquility within our soul that will radiate outwardly.

Let me give you some examples, (Quora.com)

1. Emotional Stability: people who are at peace with themselves tend to exhibit emotional stability. They are generally calm, composed, and they are able to manage their emotions effectively. EVEN IN CHALLENGING SITUATIONS

2. Mindfulness: Those at peace within themselves tend to live in the present moment and practice mindfulness. They are able to let go of the past GRIEVANCES and WORRIES of the future, focusing on the here and now.

3. Healthy Boundaries: those that are at peace with themselves are often able to set healthy boundaries in the

relationships and prioritize their own well-being without feeling guilty.

4. Purpose and Meaning: individuals who have found inner peace, often had a sense of purpose in their lives. They have a clear sense of direction and are aligned with their VALUES and BELIEFS.

5. Radiating Calmness: individuals who are at peace with themselves, often exude a sense of calmness and tranquility. Their presence is soothing and comforting to others.

Isaiah 26:3 says, you will keep him in perfect peace, whose mind is stayed on You, because he trusts in you. (NKJV).

Our belief system has to change over to a place of trust in him or we will fall into despair with those issues we have no control over by tormenting ourselves, making ourselves sick, sinking into depression. Allowing these elements to rule our lives.

Cling to the peace that surpasses all understanding that will become tangible evidence like those examples given above.

I learned a lot from my past and one thing for sure I trusted in everything else but the one who died to save my soul. (Jesus)

It was easy to put my trust in a whole lot of things, men, drugs, alcohol, money until it all let me down. What wasn't easy is putting my trust in someone I couldn't see yet I was willing because everything else failed me.

A life can be broken into a million pieces and his perfect peace can still bring A deep serenity within you that will consume you with an assurance from within that leaves you convinced everything is going to be ok no matter what it appears like.

Where the sigh turns to relief and the dread turns to anticipation.

John 14:27 says: peace I leave with you, my peace I give to you; not as the world gives do I give to you. Let not your hearts be troubled neither let it be afraid. (NKJV).

There is beautiful news! We don't have to fill the voids with all the temporary things that bring peace for a short period of time.

Eventually every false filler can bring more devastating results.

The most powerful individual is the one who can silence their inner turmoil even when the storm is still raging within.

This person has found an inner strength beyond comprehension.

We all have the power to choose so either we are going to live in peace or be ruled by distress.

Don't get stuck in a chapter that doesn't allow you to grow.

I have outgrown those chapters 1 thru 7 praise God!

I took hold of the truth and realized my past defeats cannot define my future.

No one has the power to write your story. But you!

Transformation and renewal are a big key to your peace because you can't become all God has created you to be with the old mindsets, behaviors, attitudes that kept you from being you from the very beginning.

Let me say it this way I couldn't continue to live a destructive lifestyle fueled with all the voices in mind and heart. Rehearing my past over and over and proclaiming to be free. That is impossible and the two will never mix.

We are meant to live in true freedom.

I want to leave you with some examples that will help keep your peace.

1. Prayer: When you find yourself in a place That is overwhelming that you can't control slow down and take some time to pray. Philippians 4:6 says, "Do not be anxious about anything, but in everything through prayer and supplication with Thanksgiving, let your request be made known to God."

2. Remove Distractions: In a horse race they will put blinders on the horses so they don't become distracted by what's going on all around them. Removing or limiting the distraction helps us refresh.

3. The word of God (Bible): God realigns us to his truth that gives us hope, clarity, comfort, giving us his perfect peace. 2 Thessalonians 3:16 says, now may the Lord of peace himself, give you peace at all times and in every way, the Lord be with you all.

4. Thankfulness: Reminding yourself that your cup is half full and not have empty. We tend to focus on what we don't have instead of being thankful for the blessings no matter how small we feel they are.

5. Being still: A time of quietness and listening. This has nothing to do with an environment although it is encouraged to Sit by the ocean, take a walk-in peaceful place. Being still

means to let go of every racing, gripping thought so that you can learn to listen. The Lord wants to speak to you.

Insanity is repeating the same things over and over expecting different results. We know when we are consumed by the mistreatment, the past, the divorce, financial stress there are many problems that can keep us boggled up but today choose wisely to take the steps like above to keep you and strengthen you remembering if there is no peace, there is no God. This will be the evidence that something is not aligned to his perfect word. (The Bible)

Keeping us steadfast as we trust in Jesus.

Reflection Questions

1. What does peace mean to you? (In your own words) .
2. What is the opposite of peace?
3. How is the peace of God different?
4. What were the disciples governed by in Mathew 8:23-25? How can you relate this to your life in the past or present?
5. What are some things you can do to stay in peace ?

"The peace I found through my relationship with God revealed another powerful truth—only He can truly transform hearts. This realization changed not only my perspective but also my approach to life's challenges."

Chapter 9

Only God can change the heart of man

Ecclesiastes 3:11

He has made everything beautiful in its time. Also, He has put eternity in their hearts, except that no one can find out the work that God does from beginning to end.

My mom spent many years trying to help me in the beginning when I was young. Trying to do everything in her power to get me the help to be changed. The only problem was that my need wasn't a physical issue, it was a heart issue.

There was truly nothing she could have done for me at that time. I was now a living reflection of all I had endured and bundled up as a child and my unhealthy rebellious behaviors were the reality at that present moment.

I can't imagine how terrifying it was for her not to be able to reach my heart and how could she, if it was hardened and darkened by the layers of painful broken images unrepairable through her eyes and probably to many others, my life would be classified as a statistic less likely to survive.

Her fears and tears were one day met by someone she worked with, who could see the pain behind her smile and eventually offered her an invitation to meet a man named Jesus, who wanted to give her peace.

Reluctant at first, she politely said, "I do have Jesus, I go to church," but this beautiful woman didn't give up and my mom soon accepted her invitation to attend her church where she encountered something different at that alter as she released every burden and agony that was deep within her. As the weight lifted hope poured in and a consuming peace surrounded her.

My mom life at that time reminded me of the woman with the issue of blood in the Bible in Luke 8:43 this woman tried everything and spent all she had on physicians to find a cure but there was nothing that could help her, desperate and in her last attempt she touches the hem of Jesus garment and it set her free. No different for my mom, just a different scenario. She searched desperately until she made a decision to accept the invitation to experience something new and that was accepting Jesus into her heart.

So, as you can see it wasn't only my heart that needed changing but also my moms from the anxiety, fear, depression that left her in tears, over sleeping, unable to care for herself and the total exhaustion from her searching.

Until she finally touched the hem of the garment and her faith was activated and her healing process began.

Which ultimately leads her to praying and eliminating the worrying that has no substance.

I on the other hand was consumed with so much resentment, bitterness, anger and hatred that left me escaping any kind of help I could ever receive.

I want us to understand that somebody cannot be helped unless they want it.

You can have the greatest supporters, cheerleaders, the most educated individuals with great wisdom and experience, best doctors, therapists, and it will all mean nothing. Until The heart has been touched in a way where there is a great awakening where reality and facade Meet eye to eye and the realization of what someone has been doing to themselves has become undeniable but the desire to change is burning within them becomes an actuality.

The hardest of hearts can seem hopeless with no ounce of possibility. But when a true awakening occurs Now change can come in and the amazing resources I mentioned above can now be utilized.

I want to share with you a man who had a very hard heart.

Acts 9:1-9 says, Then Saul, still breathing threats and murder against the disciples of the Lord, went to the high priest and asked letters from him to the synagogues of Damascus, so that if he found any who were of the way, weather men or women, he might bring them bound to Jerusalem. As he journeyed, he came near Damascus, and suddenly a light shone around him from heaven. Then he fell to the ground and heard a voice saying to him, "Saul, Saul why are you persecuting me?"

And he said, "Who are you, Lord?"

"Then the Lord said, " I am Jesus whom you are persecuting. It is hard for you to kick against the goads." So, he, trembling and astonished, said, "Lord, what do you want me to do?" Then the Lord said to him, "Arise and go into the city, and you will be told what you must do." And the men who journeyed with him stood speechless, hearing a voice but seeing no one. Then Saul arose from the ground, and when his eyes were opened, he saw no one. But they led him by the hand and brought him into Damascus. And he was three days without sight, and neither ate or drank. (NKJV).

Saul a Pharisee was a true example of a man whose heart was so darkened, and as we read in this passage, whether man or woman, if they belong to Jesus, he would kill them and that was his purpose on the way to Damascus to do away with any believer of Christ. But the Lord had different plans and Saul is now confronted with his actions by Jesus himself having to look at himself internally. Also blinded by the light he was left in a vulnerable state to be led by the hand by the men that had accompanied him.

We, too, will have these great awakenings where we are confronted with the truth and must look internally to see who we truly are. In the vulnerable stages of life, we will often need the guidance or leadership of others because we don't know where we are going.

I want to encourage you that there is a turning point that led us to a place to be renewed.

Acts 9:13-19 says, Then Ananias answered, "Lord, I have heard from many about this man, how much harm he has done to Your saints in Jerusalem.

And here he has authority from the chief priest to bind all who call on Your name."

But the Lord said to him, "Go, for he is chosen vessel of mine to bear My name before Gentiles, Kings, and to the children of Israel.

For I will show him how much things he must suffer for My name's sake."

And Ananias went his way and entered the house; and laying his hands on him he said, "Brother Saul, the Lord-Jesus, who appeared to you on the road as you came, has sent me that you may receive your sight and be filled with the Holy Spirit."

Immediately there fell from his eyes something like scales, and he received his sight at once; and he arose and was baptized.

So, when he had received food, he was strengthened. Then Saul spent some days with the disciples at Damascus. (NKJV).

There is a powerful occurrence that takes place when the scales fall of the eyes and the heart is renewed. Saul regains his sight and his strength the only difference now is his mission has changed from being against Jesus Christ to restoring others to the truth! Converting others to a savior who restores lives.

Saul is a mighty example of how the Lord can change the heart of man.

My mission in life has changed also when Christ changed my heart.

To see others walk in the truth of the word of God. Restored from all that came to inflicted them, released from all that bounds them, revived from all that tries to suppress them. By guiding and leading them to the only one who can restore them. Jesus!

This passage on Saul brings so much hope for those who have lost their sight by the things that have hardened their hearts or the families that believe there is no longer anything that can help their loved ones.

The Lord truly makes all things beautiful in its time.

I want to leave you with one last example of that beauty in a butterfly.

There is a metamorphosis that needs to take place which means the caterpillar body needs to digest itself from the inside out by using juices it previously used to digest food this allows the caterpillar body to break down into cells that will allow the body of a butterfly to be formed.

I love the beautiful process of the butterfly because it always reminds me of the transitions in life that we will go through in order to obtain the New. We will always have to dissolve the old and sometimes that can be very painful, but the beauty that comes afterwards, just like the evidence of a butterfly, will be worth it

Be courageous and embrace the process!

Reflection Questions

1. Have you ever tried to change because someone wanted you to ? Did it work?
2. Is it hard to change certain things in your life that are destroying you ?
3. What does the process of the butterfly mean to you?
4. What is the end result of the butterfly process? Can this happen for you? Why or why not?
5. Do you believe it would be hard for God to change you or someone else ? Why or why not ?

"Understanding God's power to transform brought clarity to the nature of love. Having endured so much pain, I came to appreciate the profound beauty of true, unconditional love."

Chapter 10

When you have experienced what love is not, you will appreciate what love is!

1 John 4:19

We love Him because he first loved us.

Love is such a vague word now days that is used so loosely by many until they understand the depths of what love really means. In this superficial world Love can be based on sex, how much you can give someone monetarily or how much you do for someone.

In no way am I telling anyone to lower their expectations or values but don't let this be the bases of how much someone loves you Life brings so many changes and if someone can no longer give you the big house, fancy car, designer clothes more than likely you won't feel loved.

Jesus is the best example of what real love is and although some might exhibit love to some degree or another no one has accomplished that pure love that Christ has exhibited on the cross.

His love was the ultimate selfless act with nothing in return only that we accept his him as Savior. (John 3:16)

He gave his life for a people that didn't even accept him just like today when the invitation goes out to receive Jesus into their heart many turn away and keep

Luke 23:20-21 says, Pilot, therefore, wishing to release Jesus, again called out to them. But they shouted, saying, "Crucify Him, crucify Him!" (NKJV).

Yet when he endured the cross Jesus cried out forgive them for, they know not what they do. (Luke 23:34)

I can truly testify that I have experienced what love is not by all my experiences given to you in this book and I am sure at some point in your life you knew what it felt to be unloved in some way.

I can guarantee our responses were far from what Jesus portrayed. It hurts to know that you are not loved so I can assure you that I never once thought in those days to love or forgive those who had or were hurting me. No! I was the total opposite! With no ounce of forgiveness. So, this may help us see that the love Jesus gives supersedes our human intelligence.

Until we have tasted of his love.

In Luke 7 the sinful woman is a woman who tasted of his Love, a woman who I resonate so deeply with of where I use to be.

Luke 7: 36-50 says,

Then one of the Pharisees asked him to eat with him. And he went to the Pharisees house, and sat down to eat. And behold, a woman in the city who was a sinner, when she knew that Jesus sat at the table in the Pharisees house, brought an alabaster flask of fragrant oil, and stood at his feet behind him weeping; and she began to wash his feet with her tears, and wipe them with her hair of her head; and she kissed his feet and anointed them with fragrant oil. Now when the pharisee who had invited Him saw this, he spoke to himself, saying, "This man, if He were a prophet, would know who and what manner of woman this is who is touching Him, for she is a sinner." And Jesus answered and said to him, "Simon, I have something to say to you." so he said, "Teacher says it."

"There was a certain creditor who had debtors. One owed five hundred denarii, and the other fifty. And when they had nothing with which to repay, he freely forgives them both. Tell me, therefore, which of them would love him more? Simon answered and said, "I suppose the one who he for gave more." And he said to him, "You have rightly judged." Then he turned to the woman and said to Simon, "Do you see this woman? I entered your house; you gave me no water for my feet, but she washed my feet with her tears and wiped them with the hair of her head. You gave me no kiss, but this woman has not ceased to kiss my feet since the time I came in. You did not Anoint my head with oil, but this woman has anointed my feet with fragrant oil. Therefore, I say to you, her sins, which are many, are forgiven, for she loved much. But to whom Little is forgiven, the same loves Little." Then he said to her, "Your sins are forgiven." And those who sat at the table with Him began to say to themselves, "Who is this who even forgive sins?" Then he said to the woman, "Your faith has saved you, go in peace." (NKJV).

What an amazing Love story of his redemption. This woman knew who she was and the mess she made out of her life but also knew what she needed. And all she had to offer him was her alabaster jar. The most expensive thing she owned.

We are ourselves come broken to Jesus and the only thing we have to offer him is a broken heart and the exchange will leave us breathless when we realize Jesus has made us whole again and every part of us is filled with life.

Jesus doesn't judge by merit but by the heart that willing to say take it, it's all I got whatever left of it, you can have it. And Jesus is his sovereign mercy is standing on the other side saying I love you and have been waiting for you to give it to me. (1John 1:9)

At least that has been my experience as I came to him in full transparency and in return, he poured out his unconditional love reminding me that he died for me, created me and only wants the best for me. Something happens when you taste of his goodness like the word says in

Psalm 34:8.

Your life can never be the same.

Jesus gives an exchange of his goodness that will triumph over every rejected and unloved area. The beautiful thing about experiencing what love is not, is the appreciation you will have for those who distribute the love of Christ.

Yes, we will experience love here on earth by those we love and that love us, but when we experience the love of Christ and allow him to love on us first it will enable us to give that pure love which Christ represented on the cross.

In 1 Corinthians 13: 4-7 says,

Love suffers long and is kind; love does not envy; love does not parade itself, is not puffed up; does not behave rudely, does not seek its own, is not provoked, thinks no evil; does not rejoice in iniquity, but rejoices in the truth; bears all things, believes all things, hopes, all things, endures all things. (NKJV).

Jesus is the perfect example of that beautiful scripture; he is the scripture! And in return as we continue to be flooded with his love we are to resemble his attributes and although we will fall short of his pure love he is always there to reposition us to his unending love again, Never forgetting we love because he first loved us.

Reflection Questions

1. Define love from your perspective?
2. Has anyone ever misrepresented what your definition of love is? How?
3. Did it leave a lasting hurtful memory? Why?
4. Who is the greatest example of love in your life ? Why?
5. How did Jesus show his love for us?

"My journey through understanding love set the stage for a transformation that reshaped every aspect of my life. What followed was a profound renewal that I could only attribute to God's grace."

Chapter 11

The transformation

Romans 12:2

And do not be conformed to this world, but be transformed by the renewing of your mind, that you may prove what is that good and acceptable and perfect will of God.

When I understood what the peace of God was, I valued it, when I learned that God was the only one who could restore my heart, I cherished him, when I experienced his amazing Love, I reverence him.

In the Bible Transformation means;

Change or renewal from a life that no longer conforms to the ways of the world, to one that pleases God.

(Got Questions, Your Questions, Biblical Answers)

I would have never understood this in my former walk where my old life was ruled by everything that kept me bound.

Living convinced that there was nothing wrong with me, but everything wrong with everyone else.

I never knew that it was possible to have a life other than the one I was so susceptible to.

If I would only leave the old patterns that I was governed by, I could be able to definitely see it was possible to obtain this new life that I have never walked in before.

A journey that would lead me to the ways of an amazing God in complete freedom.

A place where this beautiful God would embrace me and allow me to see where my life really was and what it was created for.

Allowing me to one day truly face myself in every vulnerable way, where he will then give me the right to make a conscious decision to accept his invitation to let go of all the former things that shaped my life in a very unhealthy way that contributed to all the dysfunction.

Transformation isn't just for the one on drugs, alcohol or on the streets we must remember those are the outward expression of something more serious internally.

Transformation is for anyone who truly wants change from the old person that continues to drown and kill every ambition one could have in this life.

Recognizing the new you that is and has been hidden under the pain, dysfunction, excuses or any other pattern that has corrupted you in some form.

For example,

Those who want to lose weight have to change their old eating patterns that have created the weight gain and unhealthy issues.

One has to make a life changing decision that they must change no matter how hard the journey is.

The intake and choice of food must now be different.

There might even be a change in individuals in their lives for those who will help them lose weight.

A change of commitment and consistency to this new life such as exercising.

Whenever we want change in any capacity it will cost us!

To experience this transforming power that only Jesus Christ (God) can give in this case strength, for those who want to accomplish losing weight.

God is very much concerned with what concerns us even as practical as weight loss.

I want to enlighten you that God concerns are much deeper than our physical desires.

Just like he had for me. The Lord wanted to transform something much deeper than my outside. He wanted to come in as my savior and deliver me from all the garbage I had trapped in my soul and I was the only one who had the power to say yes to God!

I understood really quick that me leaving the old person that I was so comfortable with would cost me a lot of tears, separation, endurance and perseverance it was a place of saying goodbye to the old person who was created by corruption, labels, pain, betrayal, abandonment, rejection the person molded by what was inflicted on her.

Change will always hurt, especially when it is so difficult leaving a life you have been addicted to for years and not knowing where to start in this new life that is so unfamiliar.

You see I couldn't take my old life style into the new place I was walking into,

It would never work!

The old man and the new man can never agree, they will always be in conflict with each other because One represents spiritual death and the other life.

A friend once told me when I gave my life to Christ "don't be the Christian that walks on water and land at the same time ", what She was telling me was to be real! don't live in my wild crazy ways (my old man) and then go to church proclaiming I have been set free. (the new man)

Exodus 14:10–14 says,

And when Pharaoh drew near, the children of Israel lifted their eyes, and behold, the Egyptians marched after them. So, they were very afraid, and the children of Israel cried out to the Lord. Then they said to Moses, "Because there were no graves in Egypt, have you taken us away to die in the wilderness? Why have you so dealt with us, to bring us up out of Egypt? Is this not the word that we told you in Egypt, saying, let us alone that we may serve the Egyptians? For it would have been better for us to serve the Egyptians than that we should die in the wilderness." And Moses said to the people, "Do not be afraid, stand still and see the salvation of the Lord, which he will accomplish for you today, For the Egyptians whom you see today, you shall see again no more forever. The Lord will fight for you, and you shall hold your peace. (NKJV).

Pharaoh and the Egyptians represented the enemy who was keeping them in bondage but God raises up his son Moses to take hold of his call to go and release his people from captivity. Mosses eventually accomplishes this by walking them out of slavery where they were abused, misused, to great lengths. As they started their journey the people got stuck in what the wilderness looked like. They couldn't even embrace the change and were so willing to go back to the place that kept them in bondage because they knew what to expect.

Sometimes we can be the same way in our own journeys we walk into the knew with all anticipation for the best and once we get any indication that this is not what we thought the journey should look like and it is so unfamiliar not what we expected we can easily find ourselves going back to the things that held us captive without a second thought of how bad it was.

We are all faced with some kind of enemy that isn't profitable for our well being. What does your enemy look like today? Those enemies that are holding you captive keep you from experiencing the true version of freedom and who God designed you to be.

The Israelites had a hard time in the transition; they continually quarreled with Moses through the whole process when Moses was only leading them to freedom.

We can be the exact same way bucking and kicking through the whole process without understanding and realizing that if we just endure a little more, we will see the victory.

I have examined myself many times throughout these years and many times I accepted the invitation to freedom but there have also been times I fought the process to lay down an old man that didn't serve me no purpose.

Are you ready to accept his gentle invitation to examine yourself?

Are you ready to leave a life that has no substance?

Are you ready to leave a life that is slowly destroying you?

Are you ready to start loving and caring for you the way God intended?

Are you ready to make a conscious decision to say yes, I am ready to transform my life.

In that same passage in Exodus God reminded his people to not be afraid to stand still and see his salvation reminding them that they will never see those Egyptians again!

That it is him who fights for us we just need to hold peace and enjoy the process.

What does this look like for us at this time?

It means you are no longer in captivity to your fear, unforgiveness, betrayal, addictions, depression, oppression, guilt, shame and the list can go on.

You were never created to run to the world (World representing all those temporary fixes that only give an illusion of joy, peace, strength to a dying soul. We were created to put our trust in the one who died for us so we can live life more abundantly.

His word says in John 8:32

And you shall know the truth, and the truth shall make you free. (NKJV).

His transformational power is limitless.

I have seen the power of God turn hearts from, Hate to Love, Rage to Kindness,

Misery to Joy, Distress to Peace,

Intolerance to Patience, Wickedness to Goodness, Unfaithfulness to faithfulness

Harshness to Gentleness, Indiscipline to Self-Control, perfecting his perfect way in individuals lives and it doesn't stop there. When God cultivates us from the inside out, we become a beacon of light for the world to see that there is hope. We are no longer recognizable to those who knew us in our former patterns we now have become the living evidence that God has the power to transform a life that eventually becomes a ripple effect.

Ephesians 4: 22-24 says,

That you put off, concerning your former conduct, the old man which grows corrupt, according to the deceitful lusts, and be renewed in the spirit of your mind, and that you put on the new man which was created according to God, in true righteousness, and holiness. (NKJV).

You were created to shine in a dark world. Don't stop shining.

Reflection Questions

1. What does transformation look like?
2. Does transformation bring growth in one life ?
3. Who is the transformation for?
4. Why is it important to examine yourself?
5. Why does God want to transform us?

"This transformation, while miraculous, required continual reinforcement through prayer. It was through the power of prayer that I maintained my connection to God and found strength for the journey ahead."

Chapter 12

Prayer

James 5:16

"Confess your trespasses to one another, and pray for one another, that you may be healed. The effective, fervent prayer of a righteous man avails much."

There are many individuals in this world that have lost hope, who can't see any way out of their situations. Carrying burdens even from their painful past, just like I have mentioned in this book. Finding it very difficult to let go of all those unhealthy memories that open up other dangerous avenues of dark places, which can bring tremendous situations, circumstances, trials, and tribulations that will make it even harder for us to deal with, unable to see any glimpse of light or any way out with all that they are dealing with.

Leaving them with the questions:

- What can I do?
- What solutions are available for me?
- Where am I able to seek help in my darkest times of life?

The scripture above says to pray for one another, meaning we have the opportunity to come together in times we truly need help and stand together in prayer.

There is something powerful in standing together and believing for each other in those vulnerable times when we so desperately need someone to believe with us. The scripture also says *"the effective, fervent prayer of a righteous man avails much."* Meaning there is proof in the righteous man's prayers.

What Does It Mean to Be a Righteous Man?

In the Bible, a righteous man is someone who lives in a right relationship with God, others, and creation, and one who lives according to God's laws:

- **Living righteously**: A righteous man lives honestly, justly, and faithfully.
- **Conforming to God's standards**: A righteous man conforms to God's standards of right and justice.
- **Seeking God's forgiveness**: A righteous man seeks God's forgiveness when he sins.
- **Having faith in God**: A righteous man has faith in God and loves God.

The Bible teaches that no one is righteous on their own because all people have sinned. However, God bestows righteousness on those who have faith in Him.

In the New Testament, God makes those who have faith in Jesus righteous.

Romans 3:22 (NKJV):

"Even the righteousness of God, through faith in Jesus Christ, to all and on all who believe."

In this book, I also gave my mom as an example of one who didn't know where to turn to as her daughter was lost on those streets. She eventually gives her life to Jesus Christ and starts believing God for a miracle.

I do want to mention what takes place before she starts believing God through her prayers. She had to make a decision to trust God, and when she did, He manifests His glory to her through the powerful Word of God called the Bible.

His Word eventually consumed her with peace that brought her to a place of having faith—the evidence of things hoped for but not seen *(Hebrews 11:1, NKJV)*.

The Lord, in time, answers my mom's prayers for her daughter (me).

I would become the proof that prayer works as God begins to reshape my life because of her persistence in thanking God for her daughter's deliverance. Today, she gets to see the fruit of her faith and prayers as I have been set free and delivered from all that held me captive.

She stands in gratefulness at the renewed, transfigured life of her daughter. All her petitions were not in vain.

In Chapter 5 of this book, I also talked about **Hannah**, who understood the deep pain of being barren. In **1 Samuel 1:10**, it says:

"She prayed to the Lord and wept in anguish."

Meaning she came to the Lord in all her pain for a situation she had no control over. Believing, weeping in His presence, asking Him to change her circumstance. The Lord answered her.

There is power in prayer!

We are looking at two different women, my mom and Hannah, in the most uncertain and crucial times of their lives, and they both ran to Someone that is more powerful and wiser than any human intellect: **God Almighty**!

Matthew 15:30-31 (NKJV) says:

"Then great multitudes came to Him, having with them the lame, blind, mute, maimed, and many others; and they laid them down at Jesus' feet, and He healed them. So the multitudes marveled when they saw the mute speaking, the maimed made whole, the lame walking, and the blind seeing; and they glorified the God of Israel."

The times we are in today are no different than then. There are many individuals who have become *lame*, meaning whatever has injured them physically, mentally, or emotionally now has them paralyzed—strapped to a position where they are unable to move or function correctly.

In these scriptures, we know that they were physically in need of a miracle, but truly it is no different today.

There are many who can become spiritually blinded by all the pain consuming them, unable to realize it has affected their vision to see correctly. So, they live their lives in a fog because it is the pain that leads them and not the God that can heal them.

Others can become mute by the fear that tries to control their lives, or the insecurity that strips their voice from ever being heard, or intimidation that makes them feel they have been muzzled.

I am sure in Matthew 15, they probably felt hopeless in their situations, like many can today. But we must remember: *What seems very impossible with man is very possible with God!*

During these Bible times, they had the living Word of God in the flesh, who is Jesus *(John 1:14, NKJV)*.

Those in need of a miracle were able to come to Him in their crucial time of despair, and He would answer them, just like it was done for Hannah and my mom.

When we choose to have faith in Jesus and express it through prayer, we are able to experience and see the power of God still healing others here on earth today.

Psalm 107:28–30 (NKJV) says:

"Then they cry out to the Lord in their trouble, and He brings them out of their distresses. He calms the storm, so that its waves are still. Then they are glad because they are quiet; so He guides them to their desired haven."

When we cry out to God, we are allowing Him to take control of our troubles and distress, to hush those waves here on earth.

Your cry (prayer) is what comes to still the waves. Sometimes we cry out to everybody else but God! And everyone else does not have the capability to mend a broken heart, a wounded soul, or the ability to change some situations around with nothing in return except the Lord who loves you.

He is the only one who can touch those circumstances and give the assurance that everything is going to be okay.

Scriptures to Stand On

John 14:13–14 (NKJV):

"And whatever you ask in My name, that I will do, that the Father may be glorified in the Son. If you ask anything in My name, I will do it."

Matthew 21:22 (NKJV):

"And whatever things you ask in prayer, believing, you will receive."

Matthew 7:7 (NKJV):

"Ask, and it will be given to you; seek, and you will find; knock, and it will be opened to you."

Mark 11:24 (NKJV):

"Therefore, I say to you, 'Whatever things you ask when you pray, believe that you receive them, and you will have them.'"

Prayer

Lord, I thank you for every individual reading this book, I thank you for their lives and for your beautiful healing virtue flowing through each one of them. Erase every memory that has brought shame, rejection, torment, fear, depression, sadness, and hurt. Wipe every wound and pain away in the mighty name of Jesus! Giving them the strength to rise from every place that has or is destroying their mental, emotional, and physical state. Releasing every chain that has kept them bound that does not allow them to move forward. Restoring them unto you that they may walk according to your truth for their lives. Lamb of God, give them a hunger and a thirst for you and your beautiful Word that gives hope to every troubling place they have or will encounter. Where they will know you in a very special way as you pour your amazing Love, Mercy, and Grace on each one as they read this beautiful book called the Bible. I believe in Jesus' Mighty Name everyone reading this prayer is whole, healed, and restored in mind, body, and soul. They will live again in Jesus' name. Amen!

Salvation Prayer

If you have never accepted Jesus Christ as Lord, please say this prayer with me: Lord, I acknowledge that I am a sinner and that you gave your life for me that I may have everlasting life (John 3:16). Today I repent of all the places I have fallen short; take every sin, I leave them at your feet. Today I confess with my lips and accept you into my heart as my Lord and Savior. Your Word says as I do, I shall be saved (Romans 10:9). Today I make the decision to give you my life in Jesus' Name. Amen!

May your life be continually blessed and prosperous mentally, emotionally, physically, and financially as you continue to take hold of the freedom Christ has for you.

Reflection Questions

1. Are you in the situation that hopeless?
2. Do you believe prayer can work? Why or why not ?
3. What is faith ?
4. Have you ever had a prayer not answered? Did this make you believe prayer doesn't work ?
5. Why or why not ?
6. Can you believe like David again?

"As I reflect on my journey, I see how every step, no matter how painful, brought me closer to understanding the divine purpose God had for my life. Prayer not only became my refuge but the bridge that connected me to His unfailing love and eternal plan. From birth to this moment, every struggle, every tear, and every victory has shaped me into a living testimony of His grace and redemption. My story does not end here; rather, it marks a new beginning. Just as I found hope in the darkness, my desire is to share that light with others, reminding them that with God, there is always a path to freedom, healing, and unconditional love."

RESOURCES

Hotlines

Childhelp National Child Abuse Hotline

- Phone: 800-422-4453
- Website: childhelphotline.org

National Human Trafficking Hotline

- Phone: 888-373-7888
- Website: humantraffickinghotline.org

National Sexual Assault Hotline

- Phone: 800-656-4673
- Website: rain.org

National Domestic Violence Hotline

- Phone: 1-800-799-SAFE (7233)
- Website: thehotline.org

National Hotline for Mental Health

- National Suicide Hotline Phone: 988
- Website: 988lifeline.org

Prayer and Spiritual Guidance

Pastor Pompilio Lopez

- Ministry: *In the Hands of God Worldwide Ministries*
- Email: lopezpompilio@yahoo.com
- Phone: 562-347-6002

Pastor Eric & Celia Padilla

- Email: CeliaPadilla2@yahoo.com
- Phone: 714-595-4834

LeaAnn Pendergrass Ministries

- Websites:
  » calabamalebanonrevivalcenter.com
  » leaannpendergrassministries.com
- Address:
  » 5609 CR 88
  » Fort Payne, AL 35968
- Email: hollywoodgathering@gmail.com

Armondo Rodriguez

- Email: heavenlionpower@yahoo.com
- Phone: 310-560-4213

Celeste McWilliams

- Ministry: *Calvary Christian Fellowship*
- Address:
  » 409 Underhill Avenue, Bronx, NY 10473
- Email: Celestewill9@gmail.com

Faye Hartfield

- Ministry: *2 Repair the Breach*
- Email: 2repairthebreach@gmail.com
- Phone: 404-966-5451

Prs. Ismael & Claudia Rodriguez

- Ministry: *Ministerio En Los Manos de Dios (Culiacán)*
- Address:
  » Calle El Roble #609, Colonia Hacienda Alameda, Culiacán, Sinaloa, Mexico 80019
- Phone:
  » 667-131-8423
  » 667-234-2527
- Email: irodriguezchaidez@gmail.com

Pastor José García Pérez & Zayda Isabel Benítez

- Ministry: *Visión Camino a Betel*
- Address:
  » Av. Santa Rosa 2681, Conchi II, Mazatlán, Sinaloa, Mexico
- Phone:
  » 669-150-9842
  » 669-159-8610
- Email:
  » josegarciaperez240@gmail.com
  » zaydabenitez080882@gmail.com

Pastor Jesús & Lu

- Ministry: *Decreto de Vida*
- Address:
  » Cuatro Estrellas Blvd, Colinas de Sol Estrellas, Conjunto Habitacional, C.P. 22660, Tijuana, B.C., Mexico
- Email: decretodevida@gmail.com

Books

  » "Woman, Thou Art Loosed" by T.D. Jakes, 1993

ABOUT THE AUTHOR

Leandra Soto Lopez

Leandra rededicated her life to the Lord on her living room floor in 2012. She has faced many adversities, turmoils, and tribulations as a child that led her to the streets at 12 years old, where she learned to survive.

Leandra is a survivor of mental, emotional, physical, and sexual abuse. She exhibits the strength and courage the Lord has given her in her book, *No Exit!* God said, "Released!" proving that no matter how horrible the situation was, it had no power to keep her bound.

Today, Leandra's life is a living testament to God's power to transform. Leandra is dedicated to impacting others with the love of God through His powerful Word (the Bible).

Ministry and Service Highlights:

- **2013:** Leandra directed *House of Ray*, a ministry focused on restoring broken women through the Word of God, prayer, counseling, and additional outside support to rebuild their lives.

- **2013–Present**: Leandra has co-labored with her husband, Pastor Pompilio Lopez, serving various communities in Mexico through international outreach.
- **2014**: She assisted Pastor Pompilio with ministry at *Downey Manor Convalescent Home*, serving the elderly with the Word of God and prayer.
- **2016**: Leandra graduated from a two-year discipleship ministerial licensing program at *In The Hands of God*.
- She also received the *Championship Leadership Recognition Award* for her efforts and contributions to society, presented by Dr. Linda Robinson, Dr. Robin Lococo, and Dr. Clyde Rivers.
- **2017**: Leandra received the *Community Ambassadors Award* for her devotion and commitment to serving others.
- She began directing the *In The Hands of God Women's Ministry* called *"Love Never Fails,"* which she continues to lead.
- **2019**: Leandra received a certificate of recognition from *My Gathering Place International* for her work as a coordinator for ministerial events in Tijuana, Baja California.
- **2021**: She directed *Fresh Rhema*, a program empowering women through the Word of God.
- She began co-laboring alongside her husband, Pastor Pompilio Lopez, in the cities of Culiacán, Mazatlán, and Navolato, Sinaloa, a ministry she continues to serve.
- **2023–Present**: Leandra directs the *In The Hands of God Women's Ministry* called *"Love Never Fails"* in the cities of Culiacán and Navolato, Sinaloa.

- **2024:**
  - » Leandra received a *Certificate of Appreciation* for supporting the *Inspire JC* initiative led by Jackeline Cacho.
  - » She also received the *Enriching Lives Los Angeles County Commendation* from the *Inspire JC Inspire Tour 2024.*
  - » Additionally, she was awarded the *California Legislature Assembly Certificate of Recognition* for her contributions to *Inspire JC Inspire 2024.*

Academic Achievements:

- **2009:** Leandra received her Associate of Arts (AA) degree in *Child Development.*
- **2013:** She earned her *Commission on Teaching Credentialing.*

Personal Motto:

"You are not defined by what has inflicted you, but by who created you—God Almighty!"

ENDORSEMENTS

Endorsement 1

In this book Leandra Soto has shared openly her personal childhood experiences that show the reader that a life of victory is a life that in many instances has been developed from circumstances birth in pain I encourage all readers to grasp this story of pain and realize that God is able to turn pain into powerful testimony.

Pompilio H. Lopez
Founder and Senior Pastor
In the Hands of God Worldwide Ministries
AA biblical Studies/AA Drug Studies.

Endorsement 2

I am deeply honored to endorse this incredible book by my mother Leandra Lopez, a woman of unwavering faith, resilience, and love. Throughout her life, she has faced immense challenges, but through her steadfast dedication to God and Jesus Christ, she has not only overcome them but has emerged stronger, with a heart full of grace. Her love for God fuels her mission to uplift and support women and children, offering them hope, strength, and guidance. Her story is a testament to the power of faith, love, and perseverance. This book will inspire and transform the hearts of all who read it, just as her life and faith have touched so many.

Josephine Sena
CFO American Mortgage
Leaders, INC

Endorsement 3

"We have known Leandra for over 40years and we saw first hand a troubled young adolescent girl. We believe this book will help & give hope to those on drugs and living in the streets. We have seen the transformation power of God in Leandras life seeing the beautiful women she is today"

Pastors Eric & Celia Padilla
His Dwelling Place church

Endorsement 4

I Have known Leandra for 30 years, she is my good friend, my sister in Christ, and an angel God put in my path. I have seen her grow so much in every area of her life. Her story is one many can relate to, and it will touch many to the core. Many will relate to her story and heal emotionally of their wounds. Her trials and tribulations in life have strengthen her to become the wonderful woman in Christ she is today.

I Have never met anyone as genuine as Leandra, May all who read her life story be touched by the Holy Spirit.

Monica Carrillo
Teacher, Montebello Unified School District

Endorsement 5

Pastor Leandra Lopez is a woman after God's own heart, she Exuberates the heart of the Father with loving compassion for those who have no voice. I have seen this first hand.

The scripture, I Corinthians 13:8, His love never fails, is proof of restoration in her life & true calling to His Ministry.

Pastor Leandra is an overcomer and knows her help has come from the Lord. Her life is truly the work of Lord & she has many victory stories that you will read about. In her new book, you are going to see the hand of God move and restore, like Queen Esther, she has been called by God for such a time as this, Praise God.

I'm honored to know her personally for many years and have witnessed her devotion and all that she stands for in Christ.

Pastor LeaAnn Pendergrass
Host: Uniting the Nations Broadcast Senior Pastor:
My Gathering Place Intl
13351 Riverside Drive #434
Sherman Oaks, CA 91423
www.mygatheringplaceintl.com
Calabama Lebanon Revival Center
Prayer Mountain
5609 CR 88
Ft. Payne, Ala 35968
www.calabamalebanonrevivalcenter.com

Endorsement 6

I've known Leandra for years, and I've always been amazed by her unwavering faith and resilience. In this book, she opens up about her early life, sharing stories of facing incredible pressure and scarcity. But what is so inspiring is how she never let those challenges break her spirit. Instead, she clung to God's promises with everything she had.

Leandra has a genuine heart for helping others experience the same kind of transformation she's lived through. As you read her story, I'm confident you'll find yourself deeply encouraged. Her insights will remind you that no matter what you're facing God is right there, ready to strengthen you from the inside out.

Trust me, this book is going to bless you in ways you can't even imagine.

This captures the personal connection and genuine belief in the in the impact of

Leandra's story.

Dr. Cathy Guerrero
Founder / CEO
Life Builders Seminars

Endorsement 7

No EXIT! God said, RELEASED is truly the Work of the Holy Spirit, to inspire all that read it, To develop a Faith and Trust in God, that what he did for the Author of this boot, He can also do for You. This Awesome scripture based book let's you know that I can too can RISE from Trauma to Triumph!

Servant - Prophet/Apostle Faye Hartfield
Overseer of 2 Repair the Breach Healing Deliverance Min.

Endorsement 8

"Truly, I say to you, as you did it to one of the least of these, you did it unto me."

Matthew 25:40

Since I met you, God connected us with greater purposes. You are a woman of light and a mission of strength. Thank you for existing in my life.

I have full confidence that your story will build and strengthen the lives of tens, hundreds, and thousands. God has touched your ministry and touched your life. I congratulate you for having the strength to follow your calling and now share your personal journey.

I invite you to celebrate with me this work of love, the book of our sister Leandra. Her story will serve as a guide and example to understand how God uses us all as He has used the life of our sister Leandra for the divine plan of our Celestial Father.

Blessings Sister,

JC Jackeline Cacho

Made in the USA
Las Vegas, NV
27 December 2024

15470714R00069